The Compassionate
ABC
Companion

The Compassionate ABC Companion

Kate Hodges

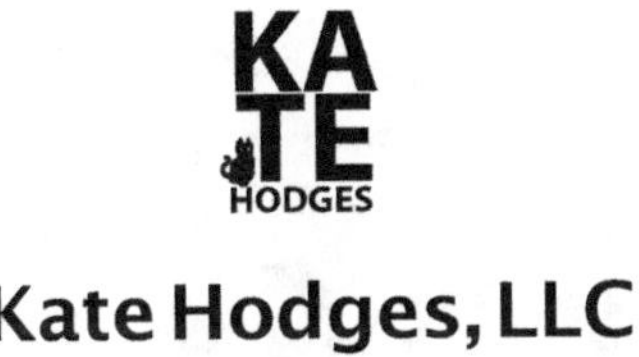

Kate Hodges, LLC

For my brothers,

Mo and Dustin

The Compassionate
ABC
Companion

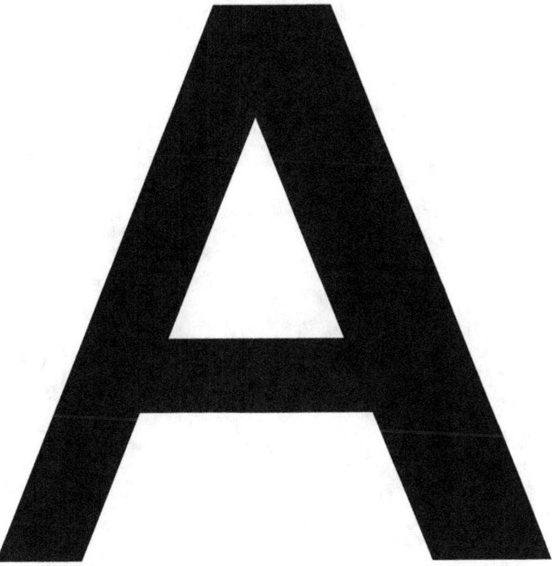

ACCEPTANCE

B

BALANCE

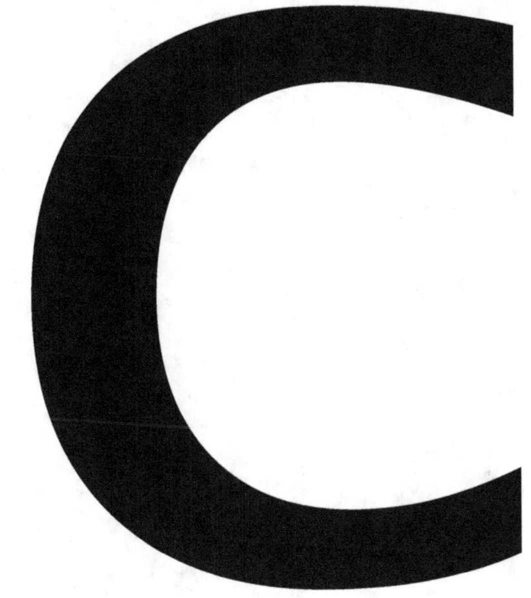

COMPASSION

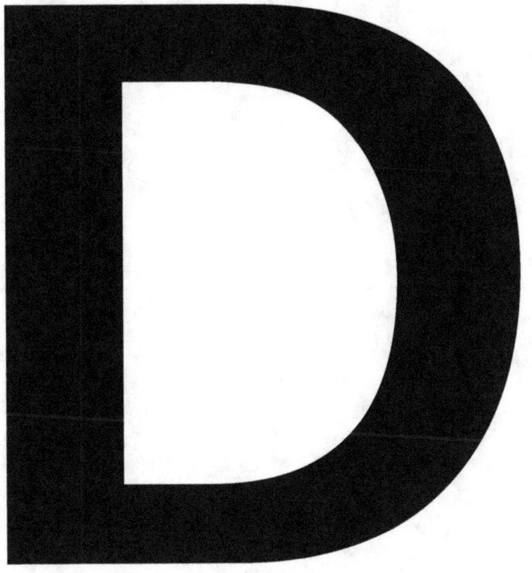

DIGNITY

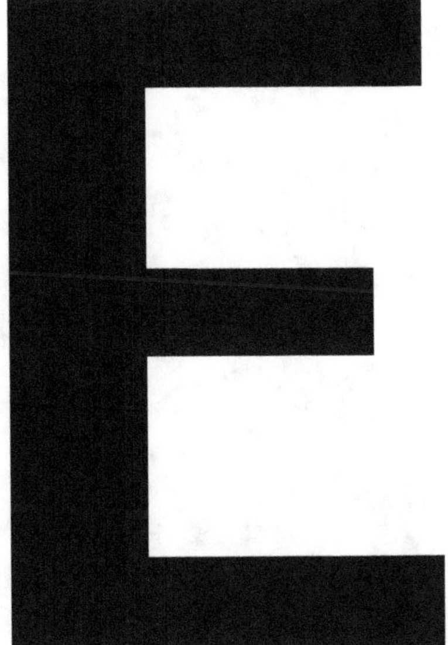

EQUALITY

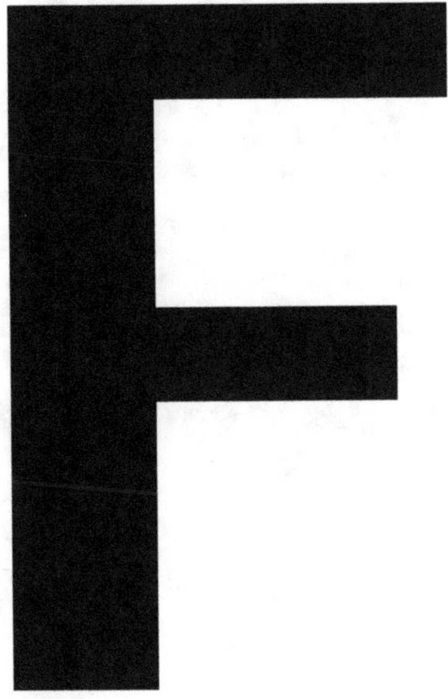

FAIRNESS

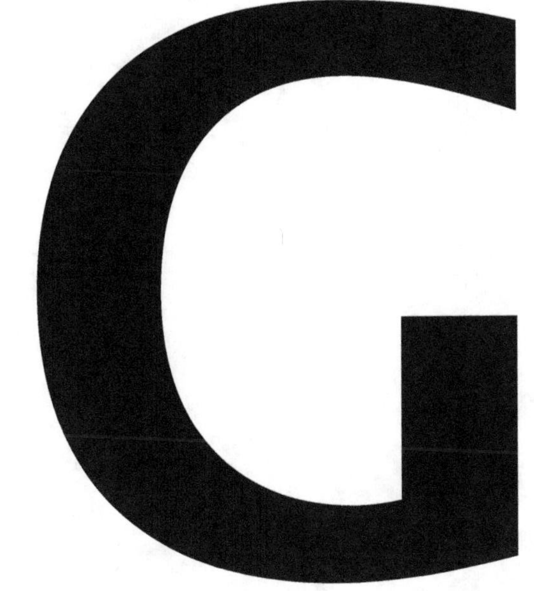

GENEROSITY

H

HONESTY

INTEGRITY

JUSTICE

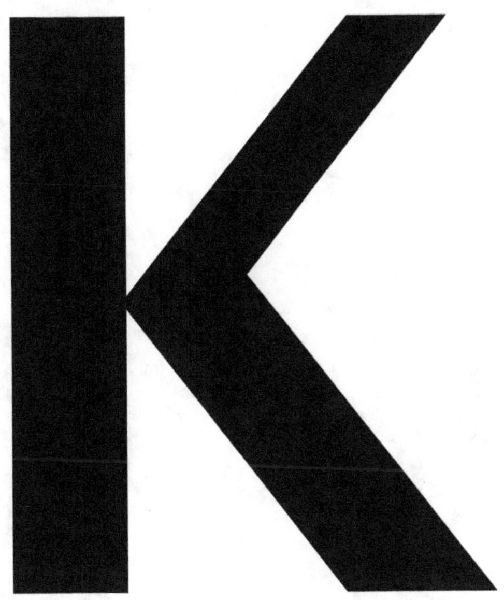

KINDNESS

LOVE

M

MINDFULNESS

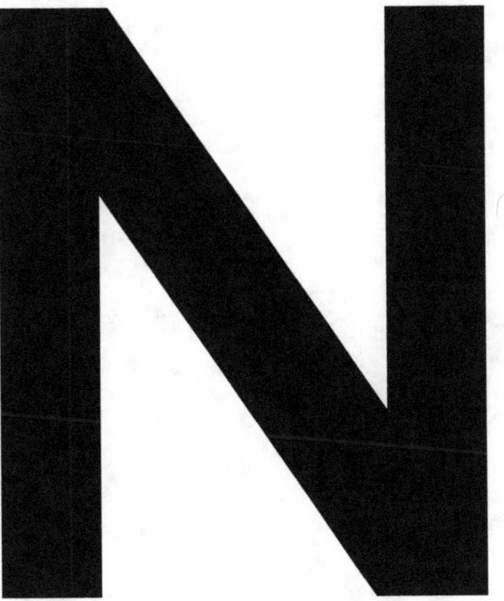

NOURISH

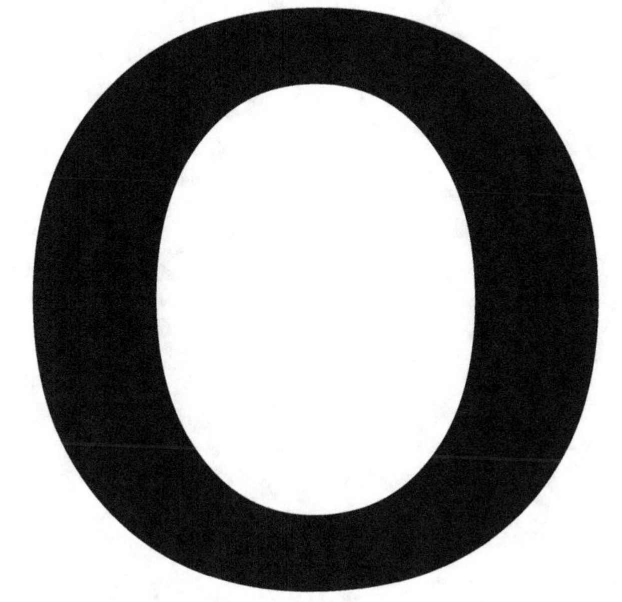

OFFERING

P

PARTICIPATE

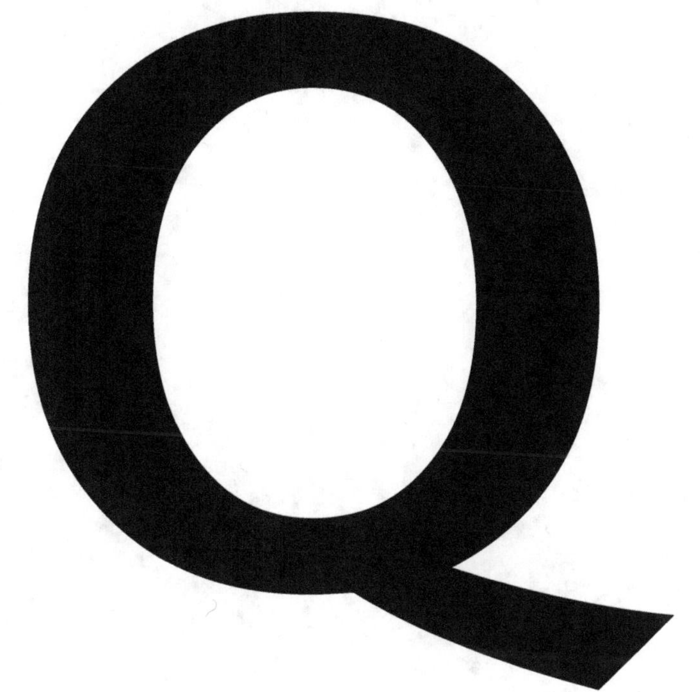

Q

QUESTION

R

RESPECT

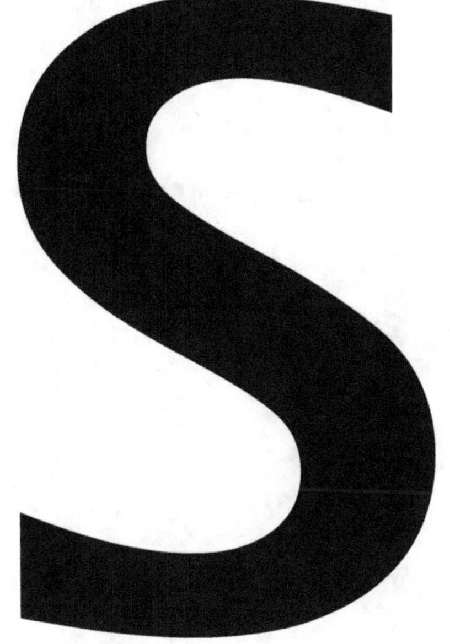

SERENITY

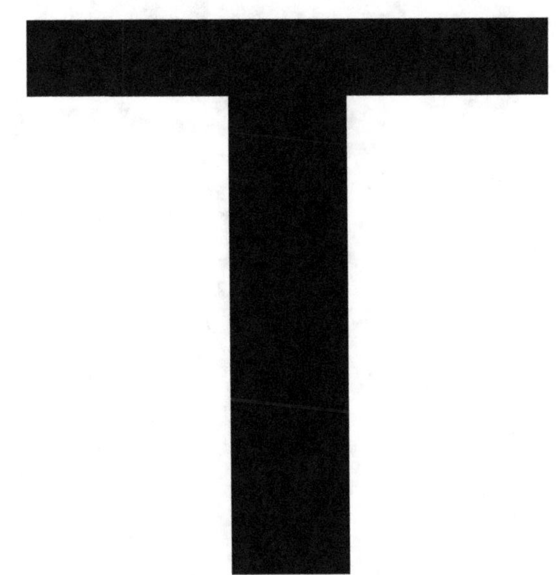

TRUST

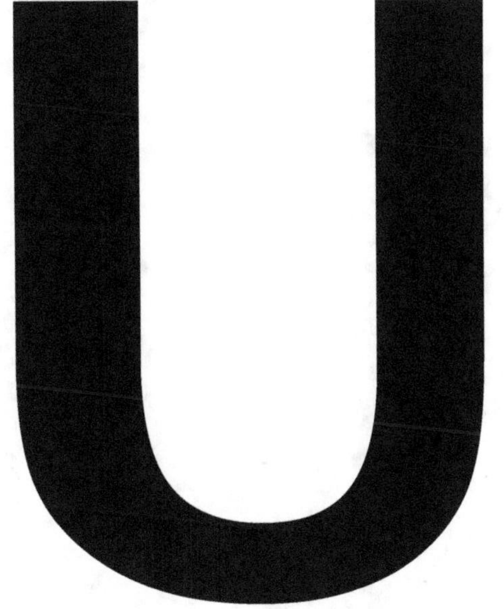

UNDERSTAND

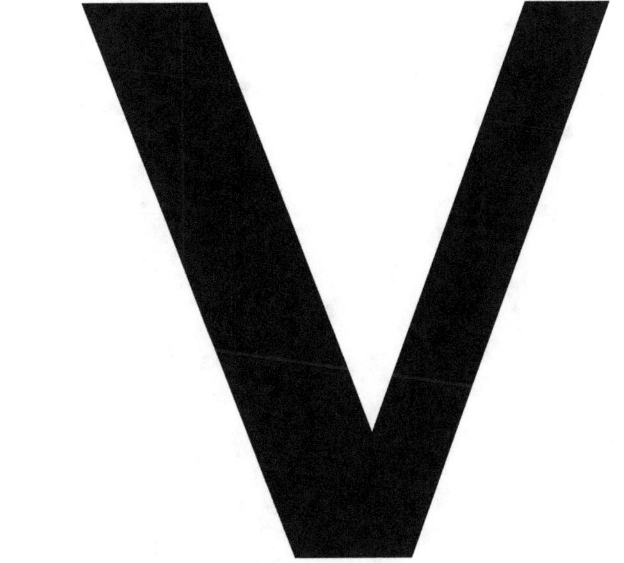

VALIDATE

W

WELLNESS

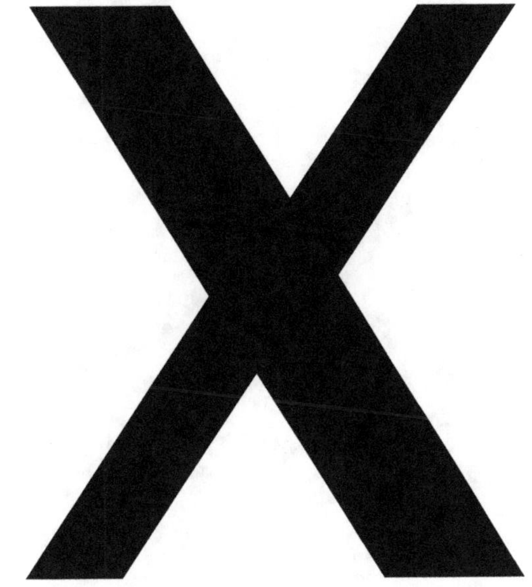

eXpress

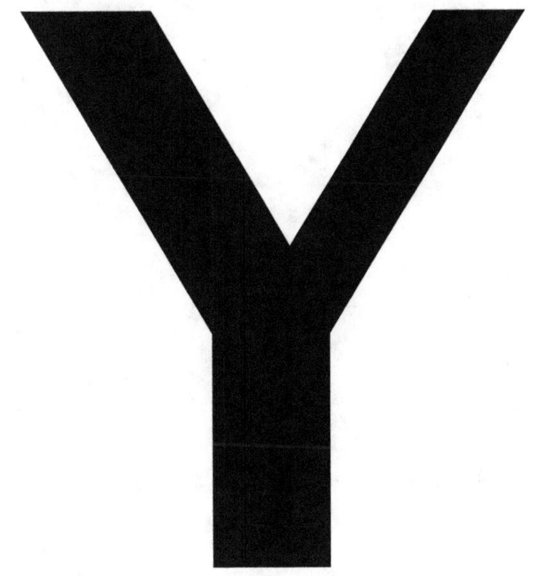

YES

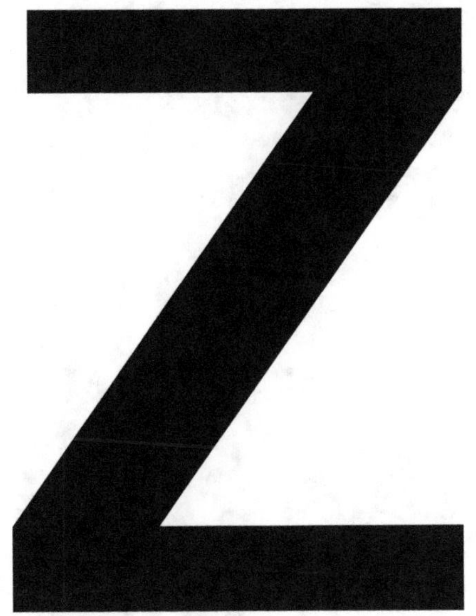

ZENITH